SAN FRANCISCO

CABLE CARS

San Francisco Cable Cars

©1994 Portolá Press and Raymond L. Wilson

P.O. Box 911, Los Altos, California 94023

Design by Bruce Estes

Art of the Cable Car

But would it work? Only hours before his city-granted franchise was to expire, Andrew Halladie and his friends and fellow-investors gathered at the top of the steeply graded Clay Street hill near daybreak on the morning of August 1, 1873. Shadowy figures standing close together in the gloom, they gazed fixedly upon the darkened shape of a "dummy" or lightweight car holding the grip and with room enough for the operator and a few passengers.

As the sky began to lighten and with a damp and chilly fog swirling about, Halladie motioned the appointed test-gripman into the dummy. Glancing over the precipice with the bottom of the hill obscured by pearlescent mists, the test-gripman expressed a sudden concern for his family and declined a descent into history. Without hesitation,

Halladie himself leaped into the car, beckoned his friends aboard, and after being pushed over the edge of the hill by several workmen, began the descent.

   As the car accelerated and emotional tensions rose, Halladie applied the grip (by turning a wheel in the first experimental model) – and the car slowed, now attached to the rattling wire rope beneath the street. Relieved handshakes were exchanged all around and the "dummy" continued slowly down the hill. Halladie applied and released the grip several more times until the base of the Clay Street hill was reached and the car coasted onto a specially-built turntable. Halladie's "wire rope traction street railroad" (as it was first called) was an unqualified success and a triumph of nineteenth-century engineering.

   Halladie's invention and the perpetual hum of the subterranean cable caught the imagination of San Franciscans and cable lines soon spread across the city's hilly street grid. Besides the ordinary citizen, the image of the cable car quickly seized the imagination of artists. Carleton Watkins, for instance, whose photographic portraits of Yosemite were already world-famous, recorded

Halladie's Clay Street Hill Railroad in operation sometime in the late 1870s.

Joseph Pennell, Whistler's friend and biographer and the best-known etcher in America at the time, paid a visit to San Francisco in 1912. Fascinated by the city with its hills and dramatic vistas, he sketched a cable car gliding down the eastern slope of Nob Hill via California Street.

Tom Lewis, a prominent San Francisco watercolorist, painted a splashy scene in 1936. The young woman waiting for the cable car and wearing a clochéd hat gives the scene a feeling for the time – and car number 789 a feeling for the place.

By the end of the Second World War many cable car lines had been scrapped for electric trollies and buses. Diesel bus companies were aggressively pursuing sales and San Francisco's mayor, Roger Lapham, was ready to phase out the last of the cable car lines, calling them "a relic of the nineteenth century".

But on the eve of abandonment of the cable

car, a resolute and feisty San Francisco resident named Frieda Klussmann stepped out of the wings and onto the stage, organizing the Citizens' Committee to Save the Cable Cars. Almost immediately she was swamped with applications for membership in the committee and San Franciscans nearly as a body set up a howl of protest at Mayor Lapham's plan.

By this time (and for some time before) the cable car had become a kind of symbol of the city--a symbol given shape in no small degree by San Francisco's artists. Louis Macouillard, a well-known commerical artist, drew his cable cars on scratchboard, a coated surface that gave a wood engraving-like effect when printed.

Probably best-known of all the cable car artists of this era was Marion Cunningham. A young and vivacious woman, Marion brought the idea of the screenprint as an artistic medium to San Francisco in 1940. Artists were enthusiastic about the idea of being able to print in colors using only inks and a piece of silk stretched onto a frame. Marion's screened cable car portraits were immediately successful and she sold as many as she could print.

Many other artists of the time were caught up in the cable car revival. Dong Kingman who was shortly destined to become one of America's best-known watercolorists was one. Another was Joseph Oneto whose hauntingly romantic paintings of cable cars by night were celebrated in Time Magazine.

The result of all this political and artistic activity saved the cable car, preserving its unique charm probably forever. And besides being immortalized in hundreds of millions of snapshots, the art of the cable car leaves us with an extraordinary pictorial legacy of a love affair with a very special and endearing form of public transportation.

Halladie's Wire Rope Traction Street Railway
Scientific American, April 17, 1875

Clay Street Cable R. R., S.F.
Carleton Watkins, photograph on albumenized paper, ca. 1880

California Street
Joseph Pennell, etching, 1912
Susan Prather Collection

A Passing Landmark – Pacific Avenue Cable
Blanding Sloan, etching, 1929

San Francisco Cable Car Celebration
Lee Blair, watercolor, c. 1930
Sally and David Martin Collection

Cable Car
Tom Lewis, watercolor, 1936

O'Farrell Street Line
Joseph Oneto, oil on artists' board, 1940

Powell Turntable
Emerson Lewis, pencil on paper, 1943

Powell at Market
Marion Cunningham, screenprint, 1944

Cable Turntable
Marion Cunningham, lithograph, 1944

California Street Cable Car
Marion Cunningham, screenprint, 1945

End of the Line
Marion Cunningham, screenprint, 1946

Cable Car Series I
Louis Macouillard, scratchboard, 1940

Cable Car Series II
Louis Macouillard, scratchboard, ca. 1943

Cable Car Series III
Louis Macouillard, scratchboard, ca. 1944

Cable Car Series IV
Louis Macouillard, scratchboard, 1944

Last car Inbound
Joseph Oneto, oil on artists' board
ca. 1948

502 at North Point
Joseph Oneto, oil on artists' board, ca. 1949

Cable Car at the Entrance to Chinatown
Dong Kingman, Chinatown, watercolor, ca. 1955

Powell Street Open Car, 1906
Evelyn Curro, colored pen & ink, 1950

Powell Street Open Car

1902 POPULAR FOR THE SUNDAY TRIP TO GOLDEN GATE PARK. 1906

Steiner at Washington
Joseph Oneto, oil on artists' Board, 1950

Hyde Street Hill

Powell Street, Nob Hill

Powell at Bush

California Street at Midday